Exploring
the Unknown

# Haunted Houses

by Susan Bursell

Lucent Books, P.O. 289011, San Diego, CA 92198-9011

To Terry for asking
To Craig for believing

These and other titles are included in the Exploring the Unknown series:

The Curse of Tutankhamen
The Extinction of the Dinosaurs
Haunted Houses

**Library of Congress Cataloging-in-Publication Data**
Bursell, Susan, 1951–
    Haunted houses / by Susan Bursell.
      p.  cm.—(Exploring the unknown)
    Includes bibliographical references and index.
    Summary:  Explores different theories about ghosts and haunted
houses.
    ISBN 1-56006-153-7 (alk. paper)
    1. Haunted houses—Juvenile literature.    2. Ghosts—Juvenile
literature.   [1. Ghosts.  2. Haunted houses.]   I. Title.   II. Series:
Exploring the unknown (San Diego, Calif.)
BF1475.B87   1994
133.1'22—dc20
                              93-4296
                                CIP
                                 AC

# CONTENTS

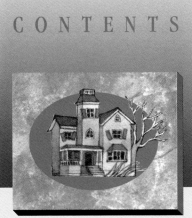

# Have You Seen a Haunted House?

Almost every neighborhood has one. Children have to pass it on the way to school or music lessons. Its sea-blue window trim faded and peeled years ago to an ugly gray. The windows are dirty and the grass is too long. In the back the once carefully tended gardens have grown tangled with bushes and trees. The house has been empty a long time. Is it haunted? Rumors say it is, but no one knows for sure.

## Important Connections

Not all haunted houses are old, run-down homes, of course. A building reported to have a ghost in residence can be anything from a huge stone castle to a tiny wooden cottage. It can be an inn, a church, a museum, or a theater. It can be centuries old or built last year. The one thing these buildings have in common is their reputation for ghostly residents.

Ghosts usually have an important connection to the places they haunt. Perhaps they lived there once. Maybe something tragic happened to them there. The ghost, or someone it loved, may have died in the building. It may appear to reenact a death or crisis. Some legends say a ghost comes back to point out buried treasure or the remains of a murdered person.

In a haunting, the ghostly spirit appears repeatedly to a variety of people over a long period of time. In fact, *to haunt* means "to visit often" or "to reappear continually." The image of the ghost returns to repeat the same actions over and over. In most cases, no connection exists between the ghostly being and the humans who presently live or work in the building.

Every culture in the world has a storehouse of stories about haunted houses. This book will explore just a few of these to learn something about why people think they have seen ghosts, what ghosts do, and why they keep on haunting.

*A medieval castle may host centuries of ghosts.*

*Sometimes ghosts prove to be hoaxes. The Hammersmith ghost, pictured here, was a man dressed in sheets. He wanted to frighten his workers and London neighbors.*

# CHAPTER 1

# Are There Different Kinds of Ghosts?

Glamis Castle in County Angus, Scotland, has an eerie history. Built in the fourteenth century, the castle has had hundreds of years to accumulate ghostly legends. One legend says King Malcolm II of Scotland was murdered inside the monstrous castle. People who visit the room where he died report feeling frightened there. The rest of the hauntings revolve around the Lyons family, who are the earls of Strathmore.

The second earl loved to drink and play cards. People believe he wanders the halls looking for his soul, which legend says he lost to the devil in a card game. One of the later earls was said to have walled up at least sixteen of his enemies and left them to starve. Visitors still hear their cries. The castle also harbors a shadowy gray lady. The lady could be Janet Douglas who was accused of poisoning her husband, the sixth earl. She was executed in 1537 for witchcraft. Visitors also report seeing the ghost of a young black boy. He was a page who was treated cruelly two hundred years ago.

The most mysterious ghost of Glamis Castle spends part of its time in a hidden room. Only the current earl and his immediate heir are allowed to know the whereabouts and contents of the room. When the heir turns twenty-one, the earl shows him the room to learn its secret.

The story is that in the early 1800s a terribly deformed son was born to the earl. He locked the child away, certain the boy would soon die. But he lived—by some reports until 1941. Villagers say they have seen his twisted image patrol a balcony on the roof of Glamis Castle. They call the balcony Mad Earl's Walk.

*Glamis Castle in Scotland is said to be haunted by a murdered king, a witch, and a deformed heir.*

## Ghostly Research

For hundreds of years people have listened to and retold stories of ghosts, such as those about Glamis Castle. But late in the 1800s people wanted to find out more about the stories. Most of these people were part of a group interested in spiritualism. *Spiritualism* is a belief that the spirits of dead people can communicate with living people. The people wanted to make contact with friends and relatives who had died. They wanted proof that there was some kind of life after death.

Some of these people were scientists. They decided to try to examine ghosts from a scientific viewpoint. In 1882 three of them—Frederic Myers, Edmund Gurney, and Henry Sidgwick—organized the Society for Psychical Research in England. Other scholars, philosophers, and physicists joined them. They, too, wanted to scientifically investigate ghostly experi-

*Frederic Myers and Henry Sidgwick wanted to study ghosts scientifically. Myers and Sidgwick, along with Edmund Gurney (not shown), founded the Society for Psychical Research, which still studies ghosts today.*

ences. Scientists who study such things are called *parapsychologists* because they study events that are *paranormal*—unusual, or beyond the normal. Since the 1880s, branches of the Society for Psychical Research have formed all over the world.

In 1953 the society published a book by George Tyrrell called *Apparitions*. (An *apparition* is a visible ghost.) Tyrrell examined all the society's records of ghost stories and grouped them into four separate kinds of ghostly appearances. The first occurs when a living person tries to present an image of himself or herself to someone who is far away. The second is called a *crisis apparition*: The ghost of a loved one who is dying or has recently died appears to a living person. The third is the appearance of someone who has been dead a long time. The fourth type appears frequently, in the same place, over many years. Its appearances are called a haunting. Glamis Castle could be home for the third and fourth types of ghosts.

*A medium conducts a séance.*

## An Ancient Greek Ghost

A Roman historian, Pliny the Younger, wrote the story of one of the oldest haunted houses. In Athens during the first century A.D., a philosopher named Athenodorus rented an old, decaying house. As he worked late one night, Athenodorus heard clanking chains. He looked up to see the horrible figure of an old man wearing chains on his wrists and ankles. The ghost beckoned to the philosopher. Athenodorus took his lamp and followed the ghost to the garden, where it pointed to a bush and disappeared. The next morning Athenodorus dug near the bush and found a skeleton bound in chains. Pliny reported that once the skeleton was carefully buried, the ghost never returned.

# New Methods

*Parapsychologist Michaeleen Maher*

Scientists today use more sophisticated equipment to study paranormal events than did the first investigators in 1882. Michaeleen Maher, a parapsychologist and research editor, uses a Geiger counter and infrared film. A Geiger counter detects the presence of quick-moving, microscopic particles known as radiation. Infrared film is special film that allows a camera to take a picture in the dark without using a flash. Maher also uses the techniques developed by Dr. Gertrude Schmeidler, a psychology professor.

Schmeidler created a method to scientifically collect evidence about a haunting. The method uses a floor plan of the haunted place with a grid of lines drawn over it. Researchers then ask the people who report a haunting to mark on the grid the spots where they sensed a ghost. The researchers also ask psychics (people who are sensitive to paranormal things) and skep-

tics (people who doubt information until it is proven) to do the same thing. Afterwards the people who toured the haunted place use a list to check off descriptions of what they saw and felt. By comparing the information from different types of observers, the researchers decide if something unusual is really happening.

Investigators have begun to use more complicated instruments. Charles Tart is a professor of psychology (the study of human behavior) at the University of California. Tart suggests that electronic sensing devices could be hooked up to computers. The computers would combine and coordinate any information the machines recorded in a haunted building. Tart has an impressive list of machines that would do the job. Ghosts are often accused of producing spots of extreme cold. So heat sensors could detect temperature changes. Infrared imagers would allow researchers to see things beyond the visible light range. Strain gauges could record unseen movement and the kind of force that caused it. Special instruments called trans-

*Researchers use the grid system to try to determine if spirits haunt a house.*

ducers would register tiny amounts of light or other energy. Electronic sensors could register and record sound at extremely high and low frequencies. All these machines would record light, heat, sound, and movement beyond the normal events produced by human beings. Tart says magnetic fields, radiation levels, radio waves, and chemicals in the air should all be measured to eliminate natural causes for ghostly phenomena.

There is a problem in all this scientific study of ghosts, according to Ray Hyman. He is a professor of psychology at the University of Oregon. He says that hauntings are not experiments that can be repeated in a laboratory like most sci-

*Left: In 1961, a Griffis Air Force Base team uses a mass of equipment to seek evidence of ghosts as a child listens in. Above: Today, researchers such as Loyd Auerbach use much more compact and powerful equipment, such as this Geiger counter.*

*Parapsychologists today use many sophisticated instruments to try to find natural reasons for "ghosts."*

entific experiments can. Ghosts cannot be relied upon to perform in a regular manner so that they can be studied. Investigators are usually called in *after* someone has sensed a ghost. So, Hyman says, "They are historical investigations, not true scientific investigations at all. . . . You must rely on the testimony of people you don't really know." Therefore the conclusions are not as reliable as those based on evidence gathered by scientists in the usual way.

Not only scientists investigate ghosts. David Stivison and John Famularo run a kind of detective agency in Philadelphia. They are skeptics. The two men say they "investigate incidents of claimed paranormal activity and provide the public with information." If someone called them about ghostly activities, they would not come in with "big equipment." They would ask a "structural engineer to explain why there were strange noises." Explanations might include such things as the building's settling or underground streams of water that cause cold drafts. Stivison and Famularo's goal is to get people "to be open-minded but skeptical."

Michaeleen Maher admits that science still cannot provide answers to questions about the paranormal. "But I am a scientist," she says. "And I believe that one day, when we have much finer tools, we may be able to get hard physical evidence for these forces. Until then, we're searching in the dark."

# What Do Ghosts Do?

Suppose you are on vacation with your family out West. You have been exploring the old mining towns and the hideouts of bandits like Butch Cassidy. One night your family stays at an old inn in a small restored town in central Colorado. The inn was built after the Civil War by William Pratt. That night you have trouble sleeping because you hear noises in the hall. You hear a knock on the door, then the sound of small feet skipping down the hall. A little girl calls for her mother. Finally, you hear a heavy thumping, as though something is falling down the stairs. When you investigate, you see a child. She is dressed in clothes from the 1800s and her hair is in ringlets. Almost as soon as you see her, she fades from sight.

Have you just seen the ghost of Millie Pratt, who lived and died in the Old Pratt Hotel? If you have, you are among many who claim to have seen or heard her. As a child Millie roamed the hallways, lonely for her mother who died when Millie was five. The stories about Millie say she was killed by a fall down the stairs.

## Odd Behavior

Millie is a typical apparition. She is usually seen at night, and she makes noises that sound like normal human activities. She skips on the hardwood floors, knocks on doors and walls, cries softly, and whimpers "Mommy." When she is seen, Millie sometimes looks substantial, like a real person. At other times she is almost transparent. She smiles, glides away after several

*Millie Pratt haunted the hotel where she and her mother died.*

seconds, and then dissolves or fades away as the viewer watches her. People who clean Millie's old room claim to have smelled a flowery perfume and felt a cold spot following them.

Ghosts who haunt have a wide variety of activities. They lock or unlock doors, windows, and shutters. They rattle or shake doorknobs and latches. They scream and laugh, moan and groan, sob and sigh. They seem to pass through locked doors or concrete walls. Most people who tell about encounters with ghostly beings say they were unable to touch the apparitions. Human hands pass right through them. Yet a few people have claimed to feel a cold hand in theirs or a tap on the shoulder. Some have sworn a ghost sat on the bed next to them, a solid weight pressing into the mattress. And in rare cases, ghosts like Millie leave a scent in the air after they pass through.

When a ghost is present, not every person in a room may see it, although they might feel a cold draft. But animals often react visibly: Dogs growl and bare their teeth at an empty rocking chair. Cats refuse to enter a room where they usually love to sit in the sun.

*Sometimes animals detect a ghostly presence when nothing can be seen.*

# A Haunted Yacht

Not only houses are haunted. A California lawyer named Lynn Hutchens claims that the yacht he bought from movie star John Wayne is haunted. Hutchens has kept it full of Wayne's awards, pictures, and books. Hutchens first saw the ghost shortly after Wayne died in 1979. It appeared to be a large man wearing a cowboy hat. The ghost also walks the boat's decks at 2:00 A.M. Investigators have found no evidence of a ghost on the boat, but Hutchens believes John Wayne still inhabits his beloved vessel.

## Why Do We See Things?

What is that glimpse of Millie visitors have reported? Most people believe ghosts are the spirits of the dead who have come back to get the attention of the living. They would say that Millie's soul stayed after death and that she is still searching for her mother. Others would say that Millie left behind a kind of mental energy or imprint on the building and its furnishings. Skeptics would say that Millie is not real—that the sighting was a hallucination and that nothing is physically there.

Why do people see ghosts? Author George Tyrrell suggests that something—the mind or spirit or soul—survives death and later shows itself. The spirit of a dead person can send out an image like radio or television waves, he believes.

*This painting illustrates a Victorian tale called* The Haunted Nursery. *Perhaps this ghostly child, like Millie Pratt, is seeking her mother.*

# Ghostly Faces in the Floor

In August 1971 Maria Gomez Pereira was amazed to see a face in the cement floor of her kitchen. Repeatedly washing the floor did not remove the image. Finally the Pereiras smashed the floor and laid a new one. But within weeks another face appeared in great detail. Workers again dug up the floor and found human bones from an old graveyard. Even after the floor was repaired again, faces continued to appear. Some say the Pereira family painted the faces on the floor as a joke. Chemists, scientists, and parapsychologists have not been able to explain how the images appeared.

The person who receives the waves creates a picture with his or her mind. This means the ghost may be an image sent by telepathy to the person seeing it. *Telepathy* is communication from one mind to another.

Eleanor Balfour Sidgwick was one of the original paranormal researchers in the late nineteenth century. She believed that objects such as furniture or buildings absorb psychic energy or impressions and transmit them to people nearby. For example, Sidgwick might say that Millie left her psychic energy in the hallways and on the staircase at the inn. Now visitors sense that energy. How clear the apparition is depends on how strong the energy is and how sensitive the receiver is. In cases of tragic events, Sidgwick believed, violent emotions stay in the room or the home. Later, sensitive people tune in to them.

William G. Roll, an American parapsychologist, agrees. He believes a person's mind can create the apparition from psychic traces left from the past. But Roll also believes a person's mental state can create things to satisfy emotional needs.

For example, a man whose wife has died may be very lonely. He may imagine that he sees her image wandering in her garden or sitting in her favorite chair. It comforts him to think that some part of her keeps him company.

Hans Holzer, ghost hunter and author, has another view. He states:

> Ghosts are electromagnetic fields originally encased in an outer layer called the physical body. At the time of death, that outer layer is dissolved, leaving the inner self free . . . for ghosts are nothing more or nothing less than a human being trapped by special circumstances in this world while already being of the next. . . . [Ghosts are] human beings whose spirits are unable to leave the earthly surroundings because of unfinished business or emotional entanglements.

So the explanation for Millie's ghost might be that she cannot leave the inn where she spent happy hours with her mother.

Are ghosts really present? Do they actually occupy space or are they purely hallucinations that exist only in the mind? Professor Hornell Hart at Duke University tells us, "If I saw a ghost in the room, the chances are that you would see it too. This is proof that most apparitions are not just the imaginings of the mind."

*Ireland is haunted by mysterious female spirits called banshees. Their wails and moans are believed to foretell death.*

# Hallucinations?

But Terence Hines does not agree. Hines is a professor of psychology at Pace University in New York and the author of a book called *Pseudoscience and the Paranormal*. He believes people are honest about what they *think* they see, but that when they see a ghost, they are hallucinating. "Ghosts are usually spotted at night," he says. "After going to bed, people fall into a sort of in-between state. . . . They are neither fully awake nor fully asleep." During this time people have a special kind of hallucination. These hallucinations, unlike dreams, seem real. "A similar type of hallucination can occur upon waking up," he says.

*Are "ghosts" the results of a special kind of dream?*

Another psychology professor who has studied paranormal experiences is James Alcock of York University in Toronto, Canada. He gives a different explanation for seeing ghosts. "I think a belief system that we develop as children . . . can lead us to think we've seen or heard things." He adds that he does not believe in ghosts. He thinks that in most cases people see what they expect to see.

Alcock might say that Harriet Tarbox is someone who sees ghosts because she expects to see them. Tarbox is an elderly lady who lived for years in a house in South Carolina. The area is famous for its ghosts. In fact, every October there are tours of plantations and graveyards that are centuries old and supposed to be haunted. People who live there grow up hearing, and believing in, ghost stories. The home where Tarbox lived was built in 1740. Local residents believe it is haunted by a woman who signals her lover with a lamp in a window. Tarbox says about the ghosts, "I saw something. I would hate for anyone to take the ghost away by saying I imagined it all. But I'm not sure if I did or I didn't. You know, sometimes memories and ghosts look alike."

*Desolate cemeteries like this one seem especially likely to be haunted.*

# Real Haunted Houses?

For as long as people have believed in ghosts some have believed there are natural explanations for them. Sometimes investigators are able to find the causes that make houses appear haunted. But often people can discover *no* logical explanation for the hauntings they witness. Here are three such stories.

## Bisham Abbey

Bisham Abbey, like Glamis Castle, has a long history of strange events. The abbey is on the Thames River, not far from London, England. Religious groups used it for several centuries. But by the 1500s it had become the family home of Sir Thomas Hoby and his wife, Dame Elizabeth. Both were brilliant scholars who expected excellence from their five children. Sadly, the youngest, William, was a slow learner who wrote his lessons sloppily.

In one version of the story, Elizabeth became so enraged one day by William's messy copybooks that she beat him to death. In another version she punished him by locking him in a closet. Then, forgetting about him, she went off to London, and he died.

People report seeing both little William's ghost and his mother's wandering the abbey. Dame Elizabeth is said to glide from room to room with a basin floating ahead of her. She is trying to wash blood from her hands. A British admiral who owned the abbey in the nineteenth century saw Dame Elizabeth. He said that she looked like a photographic negative as she passed by him and vanished.

*Bisham Abbey in England has a history of violence and hauntings.*

Today the government owns the building. It is used as a national recreation center. Wall knockings, doors that mysteriously open on their own, and footsteps of unseen walkers haunt one room. Apparently those who work there take the ghosts in stride.

Why do people see these ghosts? Skeptics say it is because they have heard the legend and have seen the picture of Dame Elizabeth that hangs in the building. Visitors might be affected by the story. They may just want to see a ghost. People who work in the building say the noises are part of the natural settling of an ancient structure. The wood and metal contract and expand with the heat and cold, making groaning and creaking noises. Others say the guilt and pain that Lady Hoby and her son left in their home have a lasting energy.

## Garden Reach House

One of the best documented haunting cases is that of Garden Reach House in Cheltenham, England. In June 1882, Rosina Despard, oldest daughter of Capt. F. W. Despard, was the first to see a strange woman in black. Rosina was a medical student, which was very unusual for a woman at that time. She was said to be a serious, intelligent woman with a scientific mind. Once the haunting began, she kept a detailed journal.

Rosina first heard someone passing her bedroom door one evening. When she looked into the hallway she saw "a tall lady, dressed in black, standing at the head of the stairs." The figure's dress was "of a soft woolen material, judging from the slight sound in moving. The face was hidden by a handkerchief held in the right hand." The woman was wearing a widow's dress and a veil, Rosina reported.

*A mysterious woman dressed in black haunted the home of Rosina Despard.*

Frederic Myers of the Society for Psychical Research heard of Rosina's experiences. He personally went to Garden Reach to investigate and interview witnesses. Myers became convinced that something unusual was happening there. He enlisted Rosina to continue her inquiry and to try to take photos of the ghostly woman.

Rosina did try to photograph the figure. But cameras at the time were large and complicated, and she never was able to do so. She also experimented with tying heavy thread across the stairs. The ghost walked right through the thread without disturbing it. Rosina's attempts to touch the woman were useless. The phantom was always just out of reach. Although neither Captain Despard nor his wife saw the ghost, more than a dozen people, including Rosina's sisters, saw and heard it. The dogs in the house also reacted to it with fear. Most frequently the family saw the ghost looking sadly out a bay window. Then it went out a door into the garden. The ghostly woman walked through the house over a period of ten years. Gradually she became less visible, until only footsteps were heard.

*Rosina Despard often saw the ghostly lady gazing sadly out a bay window.*

*This ghostly photo is said to show the Brown Lady of Raynham, an English ghost. Like the ghost seen by Rosina Despard, the Brown Lady wandered the halls of a mansion, dressed in a gown and veil.*

Later reports of the woman in black occurred in 1958. Occupants of the house heard footsteps and briefly saw a woman in a long black dress, carrying a handkerchief. Then she disappeared.

As part of her investigations, Rosina sought information about previous owners of the house. She learned that a Mr. Swinhoe had built the house. His first wife died there, and he remarried. Both he and his second wife, Imogen, became alcoholics who fought constantly. Imogen left the house, and Mr. Swinhoe died there. When Imogen died in 1878, she asked to be buried near the house. From descriptions of Imogen, Rosina concluded that the woman in black was Mr. Swinhoe's second wife.

Why would Imogen return to the scene of such unhappiness? Some think she was searching for jewels her husband was said to have hidden under the floor of a front room. Others say she was trying to find her dead husband and apologize. Maybe Rosina had a series of hallucinations. Her stories may have inspired the mysterious vision for the other witnesses of the woman in black.

# Ghostly Personalities

Throughout history people have seen ghosts of famous individuals. Some claim to have seen the ghost of Anne Boleyn carrying her head. She was one of the wives of King Henry VIII of England, and he had her beheaded when he wanted to marry someone else. Other people claim to have seen the ghost of Elvis Presley at Graceland, where he lived, as well as in other places around the world. No one knows which of these ghosts might be real and which are false. But no one questions that people have mysterious experiences every day. Here are a few stories of famous ghosts.

## A Haunted Theater

*For over a century the "Man in Grey" has been attending performances at the Drury Lane Theatre in London. The phantom is a young eighteenth-century man, dressed in cloak, boots, and three-cornered hat. Actors consider his appearance good luck.*

## Haunted University ▶

*Coleen Buterbaugh went to the music building on an errand for the dean of Nebraska Wesleyan University. There she smelled a horrible musty odor, and she found herself staring at a woman dressed for the early 1900s. Buterbaugh looked out the window and saw the campus as it was in 1915. Later she checked old yearbooks and found her phantom figure—a music teacher at the university from 1912 to 1936 who died in a room across the hall.*

## The Haunted White House

*The White House in Washington, D.C., boasts several ghosts, but the one most often seen is Abraham Lincoln. His ghost has been reported to knock on visitors' bedroom doors, to sit on his seven-foot bed and pull on his boots, and to pace the floor near his old office. Most of the sightings stopped after repairs were made to the building in the 1950s.*

### A Southern Ghost

*Former president Jimmy Carter and his wife Rosalynn Carter insist that they enjoyed sharing their first home in Plains, Georgia, with the ghosts of a Confederate soldier and his girlfriend. The Carters never found a natural explanation for the ghostly sounds they heard or for the light neighbors often saw in the attic.*

*It is not only castles and mansions that are haunted. Farmhouses, such as this one and the one the Yashinsky family lived in, also are said to have ghosts.*

## Wisconsin Farmhouse

Ghosts do not inhabit only gloomy English houses. One documented case occurred in the Wisconsin countryside in 1975. Barb and Michael Yashinsky were pleased to finally have a home of their own. They purchased the one hundred–year–old farmhouse knowing it would need a lot of work. One night their two-year-old daughter Kate had a nightmare. As Barb comforted her, Kate asked if the man would come back again. Puzzled, Barb said no. But, the next night the same thing happened. Kate was again frightened by the man with his "circus animals."

The following night Barb went to bed early, leaving Michael downstairs watching television. She awoke to a slap in the face and a man yelling "Barbara." She ran downstairs where Michael was still watching TV. He was shaken by Barb's story.

The kitchen and Kate's bedroom were often unbearably cold even though the furnace was set for 85 degrees. Twice Michael saw a weird vapor, or fog, seeping under the door into Kate's bedroom. The heavy fog smelled damp and surrounded the bed before slipping away. Barb's mother suggested they have the house blessed to get rid of the ghost. But they were afraid to make the presence angry and did not do it.

One night two years later, Michael carried Kate upstairs to put her to bed. He saw a shadowy shape in his daughter's room. It looked like a short, squat man. The room was extremely cold. When Michael turned on the light, the foggy figure disappeared.

Only once did their dog, a Great Pyrenees, react to a presence. The dog had been sleeping peacefully at the end of their bed, said Barb, when it suddenly "went nuts." It acted as if it were about to attack something in the corner of the room. The dog growled and then returned to his place.

Michael and Barb were afraid to stay there any longer. A few days later the family moved out.

*Little Kate Yashinsky was awakened by a mysterious little man and his circus animals.*

The Yashinsky's house had been lived in by only one other family. The last person to live in it was a bachelor who kept to himself. He died there. A local legend had it that a penny-pinching ancestor of the bachelor had hidden old coins in the house. No one ever found them.

What explains the events in that farmhouse? The Yashinskys believe the explanation is supernatural. Michael says, "I'm a very logical person. . . . I was in a normal state. There was nothing physically or mentally wrong with me. I'm not a drinker. I don't take drugs." All the witnesses are described as stable, down-to-earth, sensible people.

Some skeptics would say that underground waterways produced the fog and the chilling cold. A trick of light, an optical illusion, suggested the mysterious man to Kate and Michael. Or perhaps someone used trickery to get the family out of the house in order to look for the hidden money. To date none of these explanations has been proven.

# The Search Goes On

"Ghosts attract the believer and nonbeliever alike," according to ghost investigator Hans Holzer. Those who investigate paranormal experiences may or may not believe that ghosts are the spirits of the dead.

Ian Currie, a parapsychologist, is frequently called upon to "de-haunt" a house. Currie is among a small group of modern women and men who strongly believe that ghosts exist and that they do haunt houses. He says: "Forty percent of ghosts have unfinished business—they won't rest until it's communicated." Ghosts, Currie believes, "are frozen in time—a ghost is a perfectly ordinary person with no physical body."

Robert Baker is a retired professor of psychology at the University of Kentucky. Although he has examined over sixty reports of haunted houses, he firmly states, "There are no haunted houses." James Alcock, another professor who has researched paranormal reports, states just as firmly, "I don't believe in ghosts for a second." But he also admits that people who have seen ghosts honestly believe in what they describe.

In the 1800s Frederic Myers wrote, "Whatever else a 'ghost' may be, it is probably one of the most complex phenomena [events] in nature." People have difficulty believing in things they cannot explain. So they continue to search and investigate—the skeptics and the scientists, the romantics and the realists. The search offers the possibility of a glimpse into the unknown. Author Dennis Bardens sums it up: "Ghosts do exist, but don't ask me what they are or what conditions cause them to appear, or why some people see them and others don't. It is a mystery which may be solved one day, but there is a great deal yet to discover."

# What If You See a Ghost?

Ghost hunter Hans Holzer is often asked what to do if met by a ghost. Should you run or stay? Should you talk to it or ignore it? His advice is to call a parapsychologist, someone who scientifically studies strange occurrences. Until he or she arrives, you should relax and be a good observer "even if you are scared stiff." And since he firmly believes ghosts exist, he says, "Remember, please—ghosts are also people, and there, but for the grace of God, goes someone like you."

# How to Make Your Own Ghost

You can create the illusion of a ghost by following the example described in a book in the British Museum Library. The large book, called *Spectropia,* was published in the eighteenth century. The theory behind creating the illusion is based on how the eye perceives colors.

Scientists are not quite sure how the eye sees color. The *retina,* at the back of the eye, is like film in a camera. When light strikes the eye it probably creates a chemical change in the liquid that covers the retina. The liquid then stimulates nerves, which send a message to the brain. The brain then becomes aware of "seeing" color.

Sometimes strange reactions occur in the process of seeing color. Scientists call these illusions. One illusion is called the "flight of colors." Stare for about thirty seconds at a frosted light bulb, and then close your eyes. You will see a colored dot that fades from one color to another. Green will turn to yellow, then to orange, then to red, to purple, and finally, to blue.

Another illusion is called an afterimage. If you stare at a small area of a bright color for almost a minute and then look at a plain white surface you will see a new color. If you were looking at red, you will see blue-green. After looking at yellow you will see blue. And after looking at green you will see purple-red.

*Spectropia* is filled with heavily colored drawings of fantastic creatures such as ghosts and witches. On one page is a picture of a witch flying away on her broom. Her face is red, her broom purple, and her cape brown. To create an afterimage of this witch, stare at the picture for several seconds, concentrating on her shape and colors. Then look away, at a plain, solid-colored surface such as a painted wall, the sky, or a white piece of paper. Once you look away from the picture to the plain surface, you will continue to see the shape of the witch, but she will be different colors. Her face will be green, her broom brown, and her cape purple.

Why do you continue to see the witch, but in different colors? When you have stared at the witch for a time, your eyes become tired of the strong colors. As you look away to the plain surface, your eyes then see the original outline of the witch, but in complementary colors. *Complementary colors* are those that are opposite each other on the color wheel.

Try it out. Take a piece of thick paper or cardboard and draw a ghost shape on it. Fill in the shape with a green marker or paint. Stare at the ghost for a few seconds and then look outside at the sky. You should be able to see the same shape in red.

What you have done is tricked your eyes into seeing a ghost that is not really there. Could this explain why some people think they see ghosts?

# Notes

Quotations within the text are taken from the following sources listed in the bibliography:

p. 15 Ray Hyman, in Cochran, *Omni,* August 1988

pp. 15–16 David Stivison and John Famularo, in Harry, *Philadelphia,* April 1990

p. 16 Michaeleen Maher, in Cochran, *Omni,* August 1988

p. 24 Hans Holzer, in Holzer, *Hans Holzer's Haunted Houses*

p. 24 Hornell Hart, in Bardens, *Ghosts and Hauntings*

p. 25 Terence Hines, in Cochran, *Omni,* August 1988

p. 25 James Alcock, in Wolkomir, *McCall's,* July 1989

p. 26 Harriet Tarbox, in Baker, *Omni,* December 1989

p. 29 Rosina Despard, in Cohen, *Encyclopedia of Ghosts*

p. 36 Michael Yashinsky, in Scott and Norman, *Haunted Wisconsin*

p. 37 Hans Holzer, in Holzer, *Hans Holzer's Haunted Houses*

p. 37 Ian Currie, in Wolkomir, *McCall's,* July 1989

p. 37 Robert Baker, in Wolkomir, *McCall's,* July 1989

p. 37 James Alcock, in Wolkomir, *McCall's,* July 1989

p. 37 Frederic Myers, in *Mysteries of the Unknown: Phantom Encounters*

p. 37 Dennis Bardens, in Bardens, *Ghosts and Hauntings*

# Glossary

**apparition:** A visible ghost.

**crisis apparition:** A person who at the time of death, or soon after, appears as a ghost to a close friend or relative.

**hallucination:** A vision or sense of an imaginary object or person.

**haunting:** When a ghost appears regularly, in the same place, over many years.

**illusion:** A mental image, or picture, that leads a person to believe something that is not true.

**paranormal:** Something that cannot be explained scientifically.

**parapsychologist:** Someone who studies paranormal experiences.

**perception:** An awareness of something through sight, sound, smell, touch, or taste.

**phantom:** A ghost; something that can be sensed.

**phenomenon** (plural: phenomena): A fact or event that can be observed or sensed.

**psychic:** Someone who is sensitive to nonphysical or supernatural forces; similar to a medium.

**séance:** A meeting at which people try to receive communication from ghosts or spirits.

**skeptic:** A person who doubts information until it can be proved.

**sociologist:** A person who studies the behavior of groups of human beings.

**specter:** A ghost.

**spiritualism:** A belief that spirits of the dead communicate with the living.

**telepathy:** The ability to communicate from one mind to another without using physical senses.

# For Further Reading

## Books

Dennis Bardens, *Ghosts and Hauntings*. New York: Taplinger Publishing, 1965.

Daniel Cohen, *The Encyclopedia of Ghosts*. New York: Dodd, Mead, 1984.

Daniel Cohen, *Ghostly Animals*. Garden City, NY: Doubleday, 1977.

Daniel Cohen, *Ghostly Terrors*. New York: Dodd, Mead, 1981.

Daniel Cohen, *Phone Call from a Ghost*. New York: G. P. Putnam's Sons, 1988.

Daniel Cohen, *Young Ghosts*. New York: E. P. Dutton, 1978.

James Deem, *How to Find a Ghost*. Boston: Houghton Mifflin, 1988.

Peter Eldin, *Amazing Ghosts & Other Mysteries*. New York: Sterling Publishing, 1988.

Larry Kettlekamp, *Haunted Houses*. New York: William Morrow, 1969.

Earl Murray, *Ghosts of the Old West*. Chicago: Contemporary Books, 1988.

Nancy Roberts, *Appalachian Ghosts*. Garden City, NY: Doubleday, 1978.

Nancy Roberts, *Southern Ghosts*. Garden City, NY: Doubleday, 1979.

Christine Sotnak Rom, *Creepy Castles*. New York: Crestwood House, 1990.

Sylvia Root Tester, *Learning About Ghosts*. Chicago: Childrens Press, 1981.

## Articles

Sherry Baker, "Southern Spirits," *Omni*, December 1989.

Tracy Cochran, "The Real Ghost Busters," *Omni*, August 1988.

Judith Kelman, "Families Who Believe Their Houses Are Haunted—Do You?" *Redbook*, October 1989.

Robert C. Toth, "Does Ghostly Lincoln Prowl the White House?" *St. Paul Sunday Pioneer Press*, February 25, 1973.

Joyce Wolkomir and Richard Wolkomir, "Ghost Busters at Work," *McCall's*, July 1989.

# Works Consulted

## Books

Charles Bailey Bell, *The Bell Witch of Tennessee*. Nashville, TN: Charles Elder Publisher, 1934.

Stephen E. Braude, *The Limits of Influence*. New York: Routledge and Kegan Paul, 1986.

Martin Ebon, ed., *The Psychic Reader*. New York: New American Library, 1969.

*The Enchanted World: Ghosts*. Alexandria, VA: Time-Life Books, 1984.

Douglas Hill and Pat Williams, *The Supernatural*. New York: Hawthorn Books, 1965.

Hans Holzer, *Ghost Hunt*. Norfolk, VA: The Donning Company Publishers, 1983.

Hans Holzer, *The Great British Ghost Hunt*. New York: Bobbs-Merrill, 1975.

Hans Holzer, *Hans Holzer's Haunted Houses*. New York: Crown Publishers, 1971.

Hans Holzer, *The Phantoms of Dixie*. New York: Bobbs-Merrill, 1972.

Hans Holzer, *Yankee Ghosts*. Dublin, NH: Yankee Books, 1966.

Louis C. Jones, *Things That Go Bump in the Night*. Syracuse, NY: Syracuse University Press, 1983.

David C. Knight, *The Moving Coffins: Ghosts and Hauntings Around the World*. Englewood Cliffs, NJ: Prentice-Hall, 1983.

Paul Kurtz, ed., *A Skeptic's Handbook of Parapsychology*. Buffalo, NY: Prometheus Books, 1985.

*Man, Myth, and Magic*. Alexandria, VA: Time-Life Books, 1970.

*Mysteries of the Unknown: Hauntings*. Alexandria, VA: Time-Life Books, 1989.

*Mysteries of the Unknown: Phantom Encounters*. Alexandria, VA: Time-Life Books, 1989.

Jenny Randles, *Beyond Explanation?* Topsfield, MA: Salem House Press, 1985.

Beth Scott and Michael Norman, *Haunted Wisconsin*. Minocqua, WI: Heartland Press, 1980.

G. N. M. Tyrrell, *Apparitions*. New York: Collier Books, 1953.

Ed Warren and Lorraine Warren, with Robert David Chase, *Ghost Hunters*. New York: St. Martin's Press, 1989.

Constance Westbie and Harold Cameron, *Night Stalks the Mansion*. Harrisburg, PA: Stackpole Books, 1978.

## Articles

Vikki Fay, "Opening a Door to the Unknown," *Fate,* October 1988.

Lou Harry, "Ghostbusters," *Philadelphia,* April 1990.

Hans Holzer, "The Reality of Ghosts II," *Fate,* December 1989.

Leonard Klady, "The Hopeful Dead," *American Film,* March 1990.

"Maureen Reagan Meets Lincoln's Ghost," *Newsweek,* February 2, 1987.

Kathryn Robinson, "Ghost Stories," *Seattle Weekly,* reprinted in *Utne Reader,* May/June 1990.

Ian Stevenson, "Are Poltergeists Living or Dead?" *Fate,* February 1988.

Frank Zindler, "The Amityville Humbug: Part I-III," *American Atheist,* January/March 1986.

# Index

# About the Author

Susan Bursell is a free-lance editor who has worked on young people's books for over ten years. *Haunted Houses* is the first book she has written for the Exploring the Unknown series.

Bursell has had only one paranormal experience. It happened on a bitterly cold January night in the north woods of Minnesota. That night, as she and a friend tried to stay warm in their poorly heated cabin, a ghostly presence appeared and neatly tucked her more warmly into her sleeping bag. Bursell has no explanation for what happened. But that episode has made her less willing to discount other people's stories, including that of a friend who moved into a haunted apartment in Chicago.

# Picture Credits